Lineage

poems by

Karen Betz Mastracchio

Finishing Line Press
Georgetown, Kentucky

Lineage

ACKNOWLEDGMENTS

Grateful acknowledgment is given to *Quill's Edge* online in which this poem
first appeared in an earlier version: "My Grandmother's Hands"

Publisher: Leah Huete de Maines
Editor: Christen Kincaid
Cover Art: Karen Mastracchio
Author Photo: Elizabeth Ferrio
Cover Design: Elizabeth Maines McCleavy

Order online: www.finishinglinepress.com
                also available on amazon.com

Author inquiries and mail orders:
Finishing Line Press
PO Box 1626
Georgetown, Kentucky 40324
USA

Contents

Your children are not your children.
They are the sons and daughters of Life's longing for itself.
They come through you but not from you,
And though they are with you yet they belong not to you.

Kahlil Gibran

In appreciation for all my ancestors who shared pieces of themselves with me but allowed me to be myself, connected but unique, and in hopes that my children, grandchildren, and great-grandchildren will always find their unique place in Life's family while ever remaining connected.

Drawing the Lines

Have you ever tried to draw your own family tree,
lines starting out clean and close,
moving in a nice vertical fashion, when suddenly
everything goes horizontal,
you're off the page with your grandmother's
nine children and their spouses?
Lines become harder to draw,
space is inadequate, angles askew—
a roll of butcher paper ten feet wide isn't enough.

Lineage—patrilineal, matrilineal—the lines
of connection among family are not so easy.
Relationships are complex,
twisted and twined through our lives,
sometimes the strands breaking.
Each poem, anecdote, memory
captures only one facet of those beloveds—
parents, grandparents, children and grandchildren.
If the recollections seem bi-polar, contradictory,
isn't that the very nature of love and lineage?

Marge and Adie

I have two bears, small and hatted,
made in Germany, dressed in buttons and berries,
that I have named Marge and Adie,
in honor of my father's parents, my grandparents.
They're not soft or cuddly;
they are well-made, if a bit stiff,
vigilant with eyes alert and arms opened wide.
I don't know how my grandparents felt
about repairing the lives of their children.
Their love was silent,
steeped in the smell of church pews.

Inheritance

Were your eyes gray
behind your plastic-framed glasses?
I think you stood around five foot five,
enough spring in your step to march
that little daschaund down winding back stairs
to do his business several times a day,
to pull the metal shopping cart behind you
to and from the butcher shop and Urbauer's bakery.
I can't recall the feel of your arms hugging me,
perhaps a sense remains of a light brush
of your lips on my cheek in parting.
Memories fade like café curtains bleached by sun.
What remains vivid is the slight tilt of your head,
thin graying hair surrounds your sweet half-smile,
my inheritance.

Smoke Screen

Mama hated those cigars,
an almost biologic extension of your mouth,
often smokeless and soggy-ended,
perhaps what kept you speechless.

What words ever dribbled from your mouth?
Did a smile once in a while turn up those corners?
Was there a guffaw puffing out in threads,
small squirts of smoke signals, your language.

Mama, a smoker herself,
should have been able to translate
that unspoken language,
that male commitment to some stoic silence.

Instead she judged you a cold fish, Pisces born,
found your aloof manner so different
from her outspoken father
that she never quite understood you.

Sequestered in your small bedroom,
looking over paperwork,
not a grandpa who tickled or teased,
you were a mystery to me as well.

By the time you became a great-grandpa,
perhaps we knew better how to see the real you,
still settled behind that cigar,
a hint of pride in the smile as you held my child.

Goddesses

I didn't know they were goddesses,
two old maid great-aunts.
I was a child then;
it takes a lifetime to recognize truth and beauty.

Seven brothers, two sisters born at the tail end,
they lived at home into their sixties,
caring for aged parents, sleeping in the same
double bed they shared as little girls.

Their laughter ever present, deep and catchy,
their bickering sisterly, affectionate, sharp,
they loved life—their parents, their siblings,
their nieces, their nephews,
their grand-nieces, grand-nephews.

Initiating each next generation in courage and fun,
screaming from a roller coaster at Riverview,
running the bases at family picnics,
hands up to the elbows in dishwater,
they never found service subservient.

Models of the Divine Feminine,
they were hefty and agile,
donning swimsuits early to reap the sun's rays,
basking and turning, no burning,
an even tan across all 200 pounds.

Whatever disappointments had clouded their life
were filed in a closed drawer of memory,
for life was now—
food on the table, family gathered round them
waiting for the next card game or whiskey sour.
Grounded grace crowned their frizzed hair.

Catherine

Sometimes I see her round face in my mind. Her light eyes
twinkle over wire-rimmed glasses that slide on her wide
nose. Her gray hair is cropped short and curled. More
often I see the smile on her face than that sullen expression
that alienated her daughter, my mother. She never talked
much, embarrassed by her awkward English and dominated
in conversation by her vocal husband. I have inherited her
name which was passed to my mother, Catherine, and down
to me in another form. Likewise, I have inherited a solitude
my grandmother owned.

My Grandmother's Hands

My grandmother's hands rest folded in her lap,
freckled and plump, still and quiet,
resting from all the labor—
nine children born, eight raised,
tending the lettuces and radishes,
chopping the ends from the green onions,
primping and praising the flowers,
pinching off the old growth—
only the thin gold band adorning one finger.

Pa/triarch

I was terrified and mesmerized
by my mother's father.
Tall and sturdy,
he stood proud in his dining room,
his eight grown children seated around the table,
the jewels in his crown.
His broken English
never stopped him from pontificating.
All his children respected "Pa".

Like mice, his fifty plus grandchildren
scattered into crevices of the house,
but I watched and listened.
I saw his strength.
So when I was twelve
and he offered me a shot glass full of whiskey,
I drank it down.

Croatian Mystique

I never really asked about their exotic names—
Nada, my mother's oldest sister,
Zorka, my mother's middle name—
not like their sisters' names—Ann, Mary, Liz.

It was part of the Croatian mystique:
lamb on the spit,
the little garden with crazy lettuces,
dark artisan bread,
walnut coffee cake—
things I took for granted.

Certainly my mother, her sisters, and her brothers
knew more about their parents' origins:
brothers and sisters, parents, aunts and uncles
left behind near the Adriatic Sea.

It was an insular family in Chicago,
never a ghost of great-grandparents,
great- aunts, great-uncles,
no one beyond Joseph and Catherine,
their eight surviving children and
their fifty-five grandchildren.

Mama's Shoes

I wanted to walk in Mama's shoes,
those three-inch heels,
stilettoes raising her to heaven,
tattooing her every step
as we rushed to the end of the block
where she caught her bus to work
and we walked on to school.

I was flat-footed, shoes never my friend.
I tried fervently to work my way up from flats
to wedgies to those elegant spikes.
I just couldn't get there, reach those heights,
squeeze my feet and train those calf muscles.
Once I settled into sandals, there was no going back.
Comfort and my own casual style was more important
than imitating the model of my mom's generation.

All the little girls on the block
adored Mama in her high heels,
all of us aspiring to walk that walk.
In the end, maybe it wasn't about those heels as fashion,
but about Mom pushing into that male work world
that made us want to step into her shoes
and rise above.

My Mother's Hands

Common and quick as house wrens,
my mother's hands could type eighty words a minute
on an old Underwood typewriter.
Her long narrow fingers went basically unadorned,
only the simple engagement ring/wedding band duo.

She wasn't much into polish because her hands
were working hands—type, groom, cook, clean.
Strength was not only present in her eighty wpm,
but also when she brushed and combed,
braided and pin-curled my hair, my sister's hair.
Sometimes the tug and pull seemed harsh,
yet over time I knew those hands were doing
the job well, grooming that kept her girls pretty,
no hair in their eyes.

Her hands could pull a Radio Flyer
filled with two little girls to the corner grocery.
Her hands made the best
lemon meringue pie and blueberry muffins.
Her hands scoured sinks and toilets with Comet,
hung clothes out to dry before dryers did the job.
Her hands loved to cradle and embrace infants,
rocking them back and forth to rest.
Her hands were the ordinary, exceptional hands
of so many mothers, of my mother.

Lineage

Modeling my mother,
making the best of all situations,
dancing like a finch, perky and full of song,
I squeak idle chatter from my lungs,
keeping hurt hidden deep,

when my real impulse is the sulky silence
of my mother's mother,
broken English and strong hands,
sitting alone in her kitchen,
stripping green onions and washing lettuce.

My father's mother wore her big-heart smile,
understanding rules, generous in her control.
Roll the bread crusts, add butter,
but be sure the plate was cleaned
before offering Urbauer's cheesecake.

I would like to believe I am myself, unique,
disconnected from my lineage,
yet every day I find my mother, my grandmothers
speaking through my lips, looking through my eyes,
beating in my heart as I squeak, strip, and roll.

Mother's Day

Guilt chafes over so many missed opportunities,
maybe more of a melancholy,
all that we fail to learn
of the essence of our mothers and grandmothers,
each of us bearing sixty percent of our lives internally,
each of us trying to understand ourselves,
so much introspection and inner dialogue
that never spills into the lives
of our children and grandchildren
except in small behaviors—playing Scrabble,
mixing black cows, buttering rolled breadcrusts.

Old Spice

Watching Daddy shave was mesmerizing,
a ritual worth imitating—
a silky mound of shaving cream
propelled into his hands,
then spread around cheeks and chin,
a razor taking careful swipes to remove whiskers,
dipping into the sink to rinse the razor,
that water becoming progressively murky
with tiny dark hairs and dingy foam,
final strokes careful under the nose and mouth,
often a nick requiring some blotting.
Drain the water.
Clean the razor under fresh running water.
All that done, the final touch was locked
in a milky white bottle with a blue ship.
Old Spice aftershave poured out sparingly
into Daddy's hand. His two hands
rubbed together, then patted his face,
confirming him as a clean-cut man.

Watching Dad

Standing at the kitchen sink,
pouring a fizzy mixture
from one glass to another,
finally drinking down the Bromo Seltzer,
Daddy modeled a behavior for me.

In my bath, I poured bubble water
back and forth, back and forth,
pretended to drink it down—
all to be like my dad.

Later I understood the ritual as self-medication.
Manic-depression, depression, any malady
of personality was little understood in the 50s,
was not discussed even with doctors.
Then folks handled matters themselves,
mostly with alcohol, Dad with Bromo.

I never quite fell into the bi-polar syndrome,
skirted the edge and lived with anxiety, but
the picture of Dad mixing a solution
to his problem is fixed and a kinship.
We hang onto life by fine filaments,
filaments that connect the generations.

Masks

I trace the line of discontent in blood:
brooding father, teary brother, distant daughter.
Despondent all, with tragic/comic masks in place,
their faces smile, addictions hidden away.

Locked behind bedroom doors,
a knife under a pillow,
fragile life trickles down cheeks,
internal fire drying their tears.

In pain,
we hide our all too human selves—
scared, needy, distant—
in self-protective isolation reaching for relief.

I have watched for a lifetime
the patterns of a family caught
in this web of bi-polar depression,
and all I have managed to do
is smile back at their smiling masks.

First Born

Self-absorbed first-born,
I knew you as my little sister,
my responsibility.

I watched you housed in silence,
sucking your two fingers, playing with your dolls,
while I wanted to lead parades down the street,
light campfires in the vacant lot.

You were my shadow;
I was in charge.
By nature, by expectation, I
was the spokesperson, so you kept quiet.

Cast in the mold, I was too young
to see we were isolated by our roles,
each seeking to satisfy, to excel,
to abandon the restraints of sisterhood.

As time passed, first-born, I ran ahead,
as you cloaked yourself in silent independence
and waved good-bye.

Dear Brother,

We were born to it,
in our blood and lineage,
cells that push us to meet every expectation,
to work hard and live hard.
Sometimes the joy gets lost
in the ongoingness of it all.

Children of the Depression,
adolescents during World War II,
our parents experienced "dreams deferred."
When sperm met egg, those dreams developed.
Passed to each of us, nurtured
in an environment of love and learning,
we excelled,

but competition is exhausting,
our own standards our worst critic.
Even when we relax,
an undercurrent of energy vibrates
uninvited, unintended, in our blood.

On the Edge

All my kids have tender hearts and racing minds,
ready to stand up and speak out
for the classmate shunned,
to bring home all the strays.
Pressure and stress of doing the right thing
pops the lid off life, scalds anyone near the pot.
Labeled manic, depressive, obsessive—
the actual disorder is passion/compassion.

What remedy exists for open hearts and minds?
Seeing the darkness and the light,
always on the edge,
a thousand ways to deaden the pain, no real cure,
they struggle to survive.
Time served, wrong paths right themselves.
Experience, the root of insight,
strengthens tender hearts, focuses racing minds.

Once Removed

Looking over family photos, I try to place myself
in relation to my father's cousins—
second cousins or once-removed?

A tooth, once removed, finds rest
under the pillow, a child's treasure
making room for adult growth.

Once removed from the finger,
the tiny splinter that found its way into flesh
is cast aside, a faint memory.

My grand-daughter is once removed from me.
Her mother is my daughter, the link
in the chain that connects and separates.

Convicted, my daughter was once removed
to prison where visitation has rules of its own
separating loved ones by glass and chain.

The pain once removed from any relationship
might allow freedom for growth,
if one could ignore the vacuum.

Those cousins, once- removed, still tug
at the corners of memory,
tiny splinters of relationship,

but the recollections of my daughter
once removed, still have my tongue
probing empty space.

My Father's Eyes

Wide and blue, my father's eyes enticed my mother,
flirty eyes, confident eyes,
blue eyes green with jealousy.

Dad's eyes saw detail, sought perfection.
Was it a certain depth of blue
that made him so demanding?

I inherited those eyes,
a lifelong source of compliments,
some of the same vision of high standards.

My blue-eyed grandson stands out in Honduras.
Already I see an impatience in him
with those who don't see as quickly,
the gift of those blue eyes, sometimes a curse.

Hair

I brushed my granddaughters' hair one morning.
The older was having rock-n-roll day at school,
so she wanted a sideways ponytail;
the younger wanted the same hair as her sister.
The older said *that feels good*
as the comb gathered up her hair;
the younger said *ouch*, but persevered.
I explained that I would have to pull tight
for the ponytail to stay in well;
the older understood, the younger persevered.

I reminisced with the younger that my mom
would have watered down every last straggling hair,
reminding her that I had lots of experience
grooming three daughters, including their mom.

I have always claimed that the real test
of self-assurance would be to shave my head,
remove the focus of so much attention.
I have not done that,
not because I lack self-assurance,
but because there is something
in the stroke of brush and comb—a lineage
of joy and pain in those strands of hair
touched, pulled, teased, braided,
that is indeed a strength that Samson understood.

Tethered—

my granddaughters laughed at the word,
something they heard on T.V.,
a funny word meant to be remembered,
held on to like a kite waving its tail in the wind,
tossing and stretching, angling skyward,
a thin line held in a small hand
trying to control the advance,
encourage the soaring,
yet not release it entirely.

So it is with relationships—a string, a tether—
hand and kite, me and another
playing out the desire to fly free,
yet never be left to drift so far
into space as to be lost,
tension always in that line.
Sometimes light maneuverings lift and grace.
Sometimes a hand pulls back on the string
fearful winds will break the tie, neither ever free.

Even so, what human hand, what human heart
would regret those tethered moments.

Born in Chicago, **Karen Betz Mastracchio** was headed for a career in nursing. When she began her college classes at University of Illinois, it was poetry and writing that engaged her and prompted her to change her major. She graduated with a teaching degree in secondary English and a minor in writing. Moving to Texas when she married, she spent the next decade plus raising four children, penning lunch box poems, and lending her volunteer support to many organizations. Once her children were on their educational path, she returned to teaching.

As a teacher, Karen updated her knowledge of the poetry of many contemporary poets as well as revisiting classics. Introduced to new forms and styles, she was excited to share a love of poetry with her students. The endless writing activities and journals reminded her that she enjoyed writing poetry as much as teaching it. New Jersey Writing Project and several workshops at Houston's Inprint expanded her experience and skills. When life slowed down a bit, she was able to focus on the craft, revising and editing many of those student shared writings.

Karen's poetry has been published in various state and national anthologies including *NFSPS' Encore Prize Poems,* and *The Texas Poetry Calendar.* Her first chapbook, *Seasoned,* was released through Finishing Line Press in 2022. She has been an active member of Academy of American Poets, NFSPS, and Poetry Society of Texas and Poets Northwest.